LIVING WITH A BABY WHO IS GOING TO DIE AT BIRTH

TAI A. DESA

All Bible references are from the English Standard Version (ESV).

To the memory of my son

CREED DANIEL DESA

who from the womb touched lives and brought me closer to God.

To my wife

AMIRA DESA

for there is nothing we cannot overcome together.

To my daughters

ALEXIS CREED DESA

and

ASHLEY GRACE DESA

so you can know your big brother's story and create your own.

CONTENTS

INTRODUCTION

To be pregnant is to be vitally alive, thoroughly woman, and distressingly inhabited. Soul and spirit are stretched – along with body – making pregnancy a time of transition, growth, and profound beginnings.

- Anne Christian Buchanan

Before I formed you in the womb I knew you, and before you were born I consecrated you; I appointed you a prophet to the nations. (Jeremiah 1:5)

Have you ever had a moment in your life when an incomprehensible event happened, and from that moment forward your priorities changed?

Have you ever learned something profound from someone who died before you could meet them?

Is it possible for a baby who dies in the womb to leave a legacy?

My first real parenting decision was made on June 26, 2015. It was a life or death decision. My newlywed wife Amira was 12 weeks into her pregnancy with our first child. We did not know yet if it would be a boy or a girl. We were at a medical clinic on a Friday morning experiencing what appeared to us to be a routine ultrasound. We celebrated and joked at the fuzzy images of our baby on the screen. The ultrasound technicians said nothing as they moved the device over Amira's stomach. In prior appointments the techs had been more interactive and cheerful. Their actions that day seemed perfunctory. They exited the room, leaving us to wait for several minutes.

Then our doctor, Joanne Quinones, came into the room. She pulled her chair close to our chairs and sat down to face us. For a split second, I wondered why she sat so near to us.

Dr. Quinones stated that our unborn baby had "a condition which was not compatible with life."

"Acrania," she called it. "An absence of the fetal skull," she mentioned.

It would lead to "anencephaly," Dr. Quinones added. "An absence of the upper portion of the brain," I think I heard her say. Her words seemed to be slowing down while my brain started to race.

Our baby did not develop a top of the skull. The baby's brain was exposed to the amniotic fluid. There would be nothing to contain and protect the cognitive part of the brain, and therefore it could not develop properly. Dr. Quinones stated that there was no known cure or medical procedure that could close the top of our baby's skull.

Acrania.

Anencephaly.

I had just added two words to my vocabulary. Normally I enjoy learning new words. Yet both of those words were dark and cold. It felt as if Death had stepped into the doorway, casting an ominous shadow over the otherwise perfectly clean examination room in the clinic. In the span of about a minute, Death had stolen a lifetime of hope and joy. Gone were my dreams of playing ice hockey with my child, spending Christmas morning opening presents, watching movies together, teaching values, enjoying family gatherings, traveling the country together, and every other magic moment life can grant us.

Acrania. Anencephaly. I noticed that I was now holding Amira's hand.

A terminal prenatal diagnosis.

A birth defect.

A death sentence.

And a choice.

We could terminate the pregnancy, perhaps even right there in that moment. We could go home and think about it. We could carry to term. Regardless, there was a good chance of a miscarriage. Death now, or death soon, for our baby. These were terrible odds. When you have nothing but bad options, it comes down to picking the best of those bad options.

Even the options before us made me wonder. Are we making a choice for ourselves, or for our baby? What if Amira and I disagreed on what to do?

Besides the haunting prognosis of death, our baby had a heartbeat and was moving around in Amira's womb. Therein was also the obvious evidence of life. That life was even more real than anything else.

I wish I could say that Amira and I decided in that room, in that moment, that we would carry our baby to term instead of terminating. We are both pro-life, so shouldn't such a decision be easy and straightforward? What we needed was more information, more time to think, and more attempts to exert control over a seemingly uncontrollable situation.

What we did decide in that room was not to terminate on that day. I knew that was the right decision for the time being.

The next several months would bring us new challenges, new pain, new love, and new lessons.

This is our story. Of choices, and consequences. Of life, and death. Of grief, and joy. Of love, and anger, toward God. Of questions, sometimes without answers.

CHAPTER 1

WHAT NEXT?

Everything now will prepare you for the next step. Don't run from adversity; lean into it with all your heart and God will make you a leader worth following.

- Andy Stanley

After delivering the devastating news, Dr. Quinones asked if we wanted her to conduct an amniocentesis. This medical procedure would involve the extraction of some amniotic fluid via a large needle. The amniotic fluid test would provide some insight into whether there were genetic abnormalities that might affect future pregnancies. In other words, this test would tell us if our baby's birth defect was an anomaly or a result of a genetic predisposition inherited from us. We were just starting this pregnancy, and now we were checking to see if any future pregnancies could have a high probability of genetic abnormalities. Also, the results would tell us if the baby were male or female.

Amira bravely agreed to this painful procedure. Watching her lie back and grimace as the needle was inserted into her navel, I wondered if the physical pain she experienced was greater than the emotional pain of the news we had just received. The physical pain was great yet temporary; the emotional pain was just beginning.

We left the clinic that Friday afternoon for lunch as planned, saddled with this devastating news that we had never planned. Amira and I were driving in separate cars since I had come to the clinic from work and she had driven from home. Driving to the restaurant alone, I pondered what to do next. Pray? Conduct research? Try to solve the problem?

There's a solution to every problem, isn't there? I had always believed that.

At lunch, the food we ate had no taste though it had nothing to do with the cook. There was a lot to ponder.

I stopped into my office and silently struggled through three consecutive appointments. In between one of the appointments, Amira called me with the results of the amniocentesis.

Amira asked, "Do you want to know the gender?"

I replied, "Yes."

She said, "It's a boy."

My immediate response was, "Little dude!"

Amira proceeded to tell me the other results of the amniocentesis. The information offered a somewhat hollow victory. Our baby boy's condition was not due to any genetic predisposition. It was a rare, chance occurrence that the skull cap did not close. Of course, this information could not save this baby. The only consolation was that if we were blessed to have Amira become pregnant in the future, then the prospects for a healthy baby were pretty good.

After the appointments, I told a couple of people at work what I had just learned about our baby. I needed to let somebody know. Then I left early and drove home to join Amira.

At home, we started conducting research into acrania and anencephaly like two master's students finalizing their thesis. We needed to know more. We needed to know everything. Maybe the doctor misdiagnosed what she saw. After all, the ultrasound was grainy and dark.

Maybe there was a cure. Or perhaps an experimental procedure at some children's or university hospital. Maybe we could convince a scientist or doctor or Nobel Prize laureate to engineer a cap to fit over our baby's head in the womb. Technology and a bunch of phone calls could save the day.

How about God? We could pray for a miracle. Jesus healed lepers with a simple touch. He had the power. If we prayed fervently enough, wouldn't it be justifiable that God would intervene? And we thought about activating our network of prayer warriors. Surely God would notice the earnest prayers of the multitudes.

Here we were: two Type A personalities diligently seeking to solve the problem. We thought we still had control. At least we wanted control, over something.

We started contacting our immediate family members to tell them the news. We reached out to some close friends next. At least we could control who we talked with about what we had learned this awful day. No one we spoke with had ever heard of acrania or anencephaly. I guess a lot of people were expanding their vocabulary that day. A lot of people were probably Googling those words.

That evening, we prayed specifically for a miracle. We believed that God could easily fix our baby's skull. I imagined the feeling of joy I would have at the next ultrasound appointment when our doctor would look, stunned, at a completely healthy baby. That would make for quite the story.

The four weeks until the next ultrasound was simply: pray, research, talk to people close to us, repeat. My legs felt heavier whenever I walked. Yet for all I felt, Amira seemed to be taking it much harder than me. After all, she was growing a life inside of her. She was a mother for the first time. And I was a father for the first time.

There was something else weighing on Amira. She would later say that as a pro-lifer, she never thought in her life that she would give so much thought to abortion. Yet here we were. Amira said that she had a newfound insight into parents who were considering termination.

What we decided just prior to the next ultrasound appointment was that we would keep going. Amira would carry our little guy to term. We would not cut short his heartbeat. There was comfort for him in Amira's womb, and there he would be allowed to grow for the next several months. The rest would be in God's hands.

We needed to be parents in an unconventional way, given that our baby would not survive outside of the safety of the womb. We needed to make another choice.

CHAPTER 2

EVERY PERSON DESERVES A NAME

A name pronounced is the recognition of the individual to whom it belongs. He who can pronounce my name aright, he can call me, and is entitled to my love and service.

- Henry David Thoreau

Our baby boy needed a name. He deserved to be known. He deserved a strong and perfect name. It was critical that we honor him and treat him as the human being he was.

A name is something you take with you for the rest of your life. After we die, our name is something spoken by loved ones when they reminisce. It is a gift, and it becomes part of who you are and what you stand for in this world. Even if you do not experience the world in the way many people do, you still can stand for something. Your life still has meaning.

Amira and I spent a few days brainstorming. We were both big fans of the Rocky movie franchise, and the larger-than-life character of Apollo Creed stood out. There was additional appeal. "Creed" means a system of Christian belief or faith. We were going to need a lot of that.

Amira and I whittled the list down to a few names on index cards. We decided that we would each write our top choice on an index card and then share the cards at the same time. We sat on the couch and revealed our top choice simultaneously. On our respective index cards, we had written "Creed."

For Creed's middle name, we chose "Daniel." In Hebrew, Daniel means, "God is my judge." We chose these names because we prayed for little Creed to pass quickly from the corporal bonds of earthly life into the loving arms of his Creator. While we lamented his potentially imminent death, in the same moment we thought how lucky Creed was to have the opportunity to be welcomed into the arms of Jesus so quickly.

Creed Daniel DeSa. That was perfect.

All that was left was for God to grant us a miracle by our next ultrasound appointment, scheduled for July 21st. Yet I was deeply conflicted, trying to balance my faith in the miraculous power of God with the realism of the science about Creed's condition. Was I praying for two different outcomes? A miraculous healing *and* an end to suffering? What did that say about my faith? What did that say about my ability to understand science and reality? I didn't have answers to those questions yet, and I decided to kick the can down the road.

We revealed Amira's pregnancy, Creed's name, and Creed's acrania diagnosis on July 8th via social media. We wanted so many more people to pray with us for a miracle of complete healing.

Amira wrote this on her Facebook page on July 8th:

We have both a happy and heartbreaking announcement. We are pregnant with a baby boy. We are pleading with all of our family and friends to pray for Creed Daniel DeSa. I am 13 weeks pregnant and he is our little honeymoon baby!:) His skull has not developed and this will be fatal. We are asking God for a miracle, that by our next ultrasound in 2 weeks Creed will have a full skull. We believe God can do this for our baby boy. This has been bittersweet for us. Thank you for praying.

Hundreds of people, from dear friends to acquaintances, told us they were praying for Creed's head to form completely. Armed with this crescendo of prayer and feeling weirdly in control, I hoped beyond hope to see a miracle unfold at the ultrasound appointment on July 21st.

It was not to be.

The ultrasound at the 16 week appointment more clearly revealed Creed's condition. While Dr. Quinones already knew that Creed had anencephaly, the ultrasound served as final confirmation to Amira and me that Creed's skull was open. The reality we did not want to accept was even more real, and the chance of a miracle faded quickly.

I guess a miracle was not mine for the taking. As a sinner, I am not in any position to expect God to grant me a comfortable life. Was I trying to control God?

So many people wanted to know an update. Amira posted this on July 21st:

Update on Creed: I am almost 16 weeks pregnant. Thank you all so much for praying with us for a miracle from God. We see many, however I want to be very careful with my words as to not discourage your faith or prayers in anyway. Please know that after our appointment today, I feel encouraged because God allowed for Tai and I to conceive. Creed is loved by so many people. He has had thousands of people pray for him which I hope has increased your faith. Our son has ministered to you (so to speak). We believe God will continue to use him to minister to you. God's love for us is so very real. His presence is with us. He knows what it feels like to lose a Son. He also knows what it feels like to see His Son healed. Our son will be healed, but not on this earth. This is our miracle. Today the doctors confirmed that our son, Creed, has anencephaly. He will have the privilege of seeing Jesus shortly after birth. (another miracle) We have chosen to carry our baby to term. It is a painfully hard path to carry a pregnancy to term when your baby's life is expected to be brief. We expect to feel God's grace each day. (another miracle) We will have pain, but also we will have unexpected moments of joy. (another miracle) We desperately want to enjoy our pregnancy. Join us in praying now that Creed's short life will bring joy to our lives and to the lives of others in the midst of the pain. Creed will be safely protected and pain free in my belly and when he is born he will be protected in the arms of Jesus. This gives us great comfort and we know we will see him again.

Did God give us a "no" to our desire to have a healthy child, or was it a "no" for now?

CHAPTER 3

THE ILLUSION OF CONTROL

You may not control all the events that happen to you, but you can decide not to be reduced by them.

- Maya Angelou

Amira and I were at church on Sunday, June 13th – a mere 13 days before we received Creed's acrania diagnosis – when the pastor called forth a couple from the congregation who had just received a terrible diagnosis of their own. Clarence and Myra Richardson were informed that the baby growing in Myra's womb had Trisomy 18.

Also known as Edwards syndrome, Trisomy 18 is a condition caused by a problem with cell division called meiotic disjunction. An extra chromosome disrupts the normal pattern of development in a baby, resulting in serious medical complications. Studies have shown that only 50 percent of Trisomy 18 babies carried to term will be born alive. Only about 10 percent may make it through their first year. A small percentage of those babies, typically females, may live into their twenties or thirties with full-time caregiving.

Even with extreme measures, it was explained the baby growing inside Myra would likely live for a year at best. Amira was only pregnant for a couple of months at the time of that church service. As the congregation prayed over Clarence and Myra in a moving ceremony whereby people came forward and laid hands on the couple, Amira and I stayed at our seats and thought how we were lucky not to be in such a position. Little did we know that we would receive a terrible diagnosis of our own less than two weeks later.

As mentioned, when we learned of Creed's diagnosis in late June we prayed for a miracle from God, imploring Him to seal our baby's skull. God created the stars and planets and everything else, so we knew that God had the power to heal a baby's head. We figured that the more intently we prayed, the more likely God would take action to save our baby. Secondly, we researched acrania and anencephaly extensively, looking for a logical solution to save our baby even if our doctor saw no solution. We figured that we could invent or find a way.

We had the illusion that we were in control, with both our prayers and with our focused action.

In our modern, secular, data-rich world, it's easy to believe we are in control. We can order whatever type of food we want when we want. We can gather information literally at our fingertips to answer questions within seconds. We can travel to any corner of the world, typically within a day's time. We have every conceivable map at our fingertips. We can talk with someone in another country at the push of a button. We can purchase any number of items and have them delivered by the next day, and then we can return those items with ease if we decide we don't want them.

We can watch whatever sports highlight or almost any television show we want after a quick search online. We can transfer money from account to account with the use of our phone. We can express our opinions on religion, politics, sports, celebrities, and anything else freely and without the fear of being arrested or killed. We have more choices, more freedom, more luxury, and more information than royalty had just a hundred years ago. We are living like Kings and Queens of yore. And we always want more.

We have more control and certainty than ever before in human history. We believe we are in charge of our destiny. If we don't get what we want when we want it, we assign blame and demand answers. We demand comfortable lives and expect God to deliver it, as if He is our humble manservant. Our relationship with God is fine when things are going our way.

Then when tragedy strikes, our world spins out of control. A perceived loss of control leads to pain. Deborah L. Davis, Ph.D. writes in *Empty Cradle, Broken Heart*:

> Three of these feelings – anger, guilt and failure – arise from the belief that you are in charge of your destiny...This sense of control is the source of many of your painful feelings. You may be angry that your baby died in spite of happier plans; you may feel guilty that you could not prevent it; you may feel there must be something wrong with you that such a terrible thing could happen. If you interrupted the pregnancy or

refused medical heroics, you may feel an additional sense of responsibility that can heighten these feelings. You may agonize over the questions, "Why me? Why my baby?" You want answers to ensure more control in the future.[1]

The paradox of modern medicine allows us to know more about a baby in the womb, yet sometimes too many tests and too much information can actually be detrimental. With advanced medical technology, a panoply of tests give us the power to identify preexisting problems in the baby and potential problems with the pregnancy. These tests can be useful if corrective action can be taken to protect the mother and/or baby. However, what if there isn't anything that can be done?

Up until about 25 years ago, doctors and parents did not know a baby in the womb had a terminal condition until the birth. Today, the capacity to diagnose problems like anencephaly gives parents heart-wrenching choices. They can elect to medically terminate the baby's life or let the pregnancy play out. Many parents terminate the pregnancy when they are told that their baby has a condition like acrania, anencephaly, Trisomy 18 (Edwards syndrome), or Potter sequence. Some medical professionals are befuddled as to why parents would continue the pregnancy.

Part of the notion of always being in control is that when something does not go the way we want, we believe that it was:

- Caused by someone else who is controlling things and therefore they need to be blamed, and corrected, or

- Caused by a mistake we made, and therefore it is something we must change, or

- Caused by our failure, which can negatively affect our psyche and self-esteem, or

- Caused by God being angry, uncaring, or impotent, or

- Caused by the Devil.

In the event of a troubled pregnancy, a woman may feel that her body is somehow flawed. Amira felt that way. I wondered what could have been done – perhaps taking loads of vitamins – to change the outcome. I felt shame at wondering what we could have done.

The truth is that Amira was worthy, and Creed was worthy. Amira did nothing wrong at any point of her pregnancy. God had pre-ordained Creed to live the life he did, a short yet meaningful one. In the history of time and the history of God, we all live short lives. We all live meaningful lives. Our lives are more fulfilling and colorful for us if we continually find that meaning. Even if we typically don't find that meaning, it is still there. If a person doesn't find God in their life, God is still there.

We all will have times in our lives where we feel immense pain. We will all know sorrow, heartache, loss, pain, sadness, helplessness, sickness, envy, hopelessness, and disappointment. If you're not feeling pain now, just wait, it is coming. The objective is not so much to avoid pain (which we all take great strides to avoid), but to prepare for pain and then grow through the pain when it inevitably comes. We prepare for an exam; we prepare for a vacation; we prepare for a date;

we prepare for a party; we prepare for an interview; we can and should prepare for affliction. Pain deep in our being prepares us and strengthens us for the next challenge. A stronger soul helps us to be unsurprised when life's circumstances are difficult or unfair. That strength we develop may be what others need so they can effectively deal with *their* challenges.

Part of being capable of deriving meaning is to be prepared for pain. Yet that is easier said than done.

An interesting thing about pain is that it gives us a close encounter, and perhaps a closer relationship, with God. When things are going incredibly well, God may be pushed off to the side. When things are going horribly, sometimes we may cry out to God and sometimes we may scream at God.

I pondered these questions:

What if my pain is God yelling at me?

What if my pain is God calling me closer to Him?

What if pain is the catalyst God sent me to make me stronger?

What if there is a deeper meaning in the pain that God wants me to see?

What if bad things are not an indication of a lack of faith?

What if my soul is so strong that I am prepared to be unsurprised when life is tough?

What if this tough time is preparation for me to deal effectively with the next, tougher time?

Many people find God when they deal with pain and suffering. Some people don't find God at those times. Some people feel that God has left them. Some people may try to leave God because they feel He abandoned them.

Per Timothy Keller in *Walking with God through Pain and Suffering*, suffering is at the heart of why people disbelieve and believe in God, of why people decline and grow in character, and of how God becomes less real and more real to us. Keller writes:

> And when we looked to the Bible to understand this deep pattern, we came to see that the great theme of the Bible itself is how God brings fullness of joy not just despite but *through* suffering, just as Jesus saved us not in spite of but *because* of what he endured on the cross. And so there is a peculiar, rich, and poignant joy that seems to come to us only through and in suffering.[2]

As July wore on, we quickly grew to accept the diagnosis of acrania and anencephaly. Amira and I could see death coming in the distance for our unborn child. Creed's skull would not miraculously close, and his brain would not miraculously grow. It was out of our control.

We could do nothing to save our child. Perhaps God was doing something, through Creed, to save *us*.

CHAPTER 4

SEIZING PARENTHOOD BEFORE BIRTH

When you moved, I felt squeezed with a wild infatuation and protectiveness. We are one. Nothing, not even death, can change that.

- Suzanne Finnamore, *The Zygote Chronicles*

Everyone knows their birthdate. Few of us know our death date. What would our life be like if we knew our death day? What would our life be like if someone else determined our death day for us?

Creed's due date was January 8th, 2016. We knew that his birth date – whether it be January 8th or another date – would likely be his death date too. Since our time with Creed was so limited, we decided to take on the role of parents before Creed was born.

Dr. Quinones told us that Creed would feel no pain while he was in the womb, and she added that he was probably able to hear us. Our fleeting moments of being first-time parents were precious as we sought to maximize Creed's earthly experiences. I became thankful that modern technology allowed Amira and me to know about Creed's anencephaly so we could seize parenthood instead of finding out at childbirth about his condition.

On July 11th, Amira and I went to the beach in Asbury Park, New Jersey. We hoped that while in the womb he would hear the crashing of the waves and the caws of the seagulls. We wrote his name in the sand just before the sun set.

On July 17th, I took Amira and Creed to the Rocky Steps at the Philadelphia Art Museum. I had proposed to Amira at the top of the steps less than a year earlier, on November 22nd, 2014.

On July 27th, Amira and I celebrated the 68th wedding anniversary of her grandparents in Knoxville, Tennessee. With Creed in Amira's womb, that made four generations of people in one room.

On August 6th, we watched a Phillies game in Philadelphia and then roamed the Musikfest festival grounds in Bethlehem, Pennsylvania.

On September 5th – Amira's birthday – I took her and Creed to Cape May, New Jersey for dinner. We went to Sunset Beach to observe the last wisps of sunlight over the water.

On September 19th, we watched my alma mater, the University of Pennsylvania, play Lehigh University in college football.

On September 26th, we attended a Billy Joel concert at Madison Square Garden.

On November 8th, we attended a childbirth class at the hospital. One of the instructors was Nurse Rachel Hoffman. Little did we know that she would be the nurse when Amira would give birth.

On November 13th, Amira and I attended the Buffalo Bills vs. New York Jets game at MetLife Stadium in New Jersey. It was the first NFL game for Creed and Amira.

On November 20th, we spontaneously attended an Air Supply concert after learning about it just an hour earlier.

We navigated our way through a maze of corn stalks; we carved pumpkins; we warmed ourselves in front of the fireplace; we spent time with Creed's grandmothers; we talked to him so he could hear our voices.

With a fetal doppler device, we frequently listened to Creed's heartbeat. Amira felt his kicks, and so did I when I placed my head against Amira's tummy. We sang to him and prayed next to him even as he lay in the womb. Whether at church or at the movies, we hoped Creed could hear sounds of life beyond his own.

I got to be a daddy and Amira got to be a mommy, if but for a fleeting moment.

We looked forward to the instant when we could hold Creed in our arms, believing that we could be lucky to have just a few minutes after birth before his body would shut down. We planned to get his footprints and handprints, take some photos, and record a few gurgling sounds.

We chose to love Creed and honor him. We wanted him to have a funeral. And we prayed. Prayed for him. For other parents who have a baby with anencephaly. For Creed to have a little brother or sister one day. For us to see him in Heaven when the Lord permits us.

What you focus on, you feel. If we focus on pain, injustice, hatred, prejudice, violence, depression, and greed, we will find that there is plenty in the world. If we focus on love, hope, joy, peace, fulfillment, gratitude, and giving, there is plenty to see and feel and appreciate. The evidence is all around us. There is a superabundance of love, hope, gratitude, and giving.

Countless family, friends, and total strangers contacted us to show how much they care. We discovered that we are part of an endless community that we previously didn't know was there. Many people privately shared their stories of losing young children. It's apparent that a lot of people carry a wound and a place in their heart for a child whose time came way too soon. Life goes on. It was, and is, comforting to sense the strength of others.

On November 3rd, we attended another ultrasound. Creed's face looked a lot like mine. He looked like me in my baby pictures. What a joy it was to see our son in those grainy images. I wanted so badly to hold him and hear his murmurs. I was sure that I would get that chance within weeks. Little did I know that my expectations would be dashed.

CHAPTER 5

CARRYING TO TERM

Birth is not only about making babies. Birth is about making mothers...strong, competent, capable mothers who trust themselves and know their inner strength.

- Barbara Katz Rothman

We spent that summer dealing with a variety of challenges, apparent contradictions, and moments of inspiration.

Some people told us matter-of-factly that we were foolish to carry our baby to term. Terminate, and move on, they say. They were mystified why we would continue with this pregnancy. In one sense, they were right in that carrying to term would prolong the emotional attachment to our baby and therefore the grief. Yet how could we stop our baby's heartbeat and deny ourselves the chance to hold our baby in our arms, but for a few minutes?

Some people told us to pray *only* for a miracle, even in the face of clear evidence that anencephalic babies do not survive. Someone even became upset that we were praying for comfort for our baby instead of solely praying for a miracle. We have been taught as kids to pray for miracles and that God answers prayers. Yet the contradiction was that we felt like we were deluding ourselves in praying for a miracle, as that would be akin to praying for a person with no arm to magically grow one. Amira and I switched from praying for a miraculous skull formation to praying for our baby to have comfort now, along with a warm welcome into the arms of Jesus soon.

Some people who did not know our story would spontaneously congratulate us when they saw Amira's growing baby bump, yet we did not have the heart to tell them that we knew our baby would die. Many people are happy to see someone pregnant. We chose sometimes not to tell people about the anencephaly diagnosis. Why should we make them feel awkward and sad when they are giving us joy? And why not share their joy at seeing Amira pregnant? Aren't emotions really a choice, and why not choose to be joyous more often than not?

Sometimes we became angry with God because of our innocent child's deadly diagnosis, yet sometimes we felt so much closer to Him because of this challenge. It was something new for us to be angry with the Lord for what is happening, yet we felt closer to God when in the presence of such an outpouring of love from family and friends. When we received kind words and notes from people we knew well and people we barely knew, we found that many of them saw us as an inspiration.

Creed's heartbeat and kicks were real. A baby with anencephaly is a human being. A person's humanity is not downgraded because of illness, disability, or intellectual impediment.

A baby with anencephaly is a disabled person with special needs. If a fully functioning person suffered brain dysfunction from head trauma, asphyxiation, a tumor, or a stroke, they would be given care.

Who am I to judge the value and worthiness of another person? Who am I to pass judgment on someone else, especially if they are unable to speak to their own defense? I believe I should not end the life of another because that person might adversely impact my lifestyle. Easing my own suffering or anticipated future suffering is not a legitimate reason to end another person's life.

In *A Gift of Time: Continuing Your Pregnancy When Your Baby's Life is Expected to Be Brief*, authors Amy Kuebeleck and Deborah L. Davis, Ph. D. state, "Some parents decide to continue not so much out of a desire to carry to term but because the alternative is something they cannot bring themselves to do."[3]

Creed was safe and warm in Amira's womb. He had nourishment. This was Creed's chance to know his mother, and for Amira to know him as best as she could. Creed deserved that time with his mother before being accepted into the loving arms of Jesus.

As painful as it sometimes was for Amira to carry a baby she knew would not survive long, if at all, outside of the womb, carrying Creed to term helped her deal with grief.

Abortion for a birth defect can negatively impact the mother's mental health. Since anencephaly and other abnormalities are discovered later in the pregnancy, the mother often has already formed an emotional connection with the baby. The notion of holding Creed in our arms, even if for a fleeting few minutes, seemed a better way to say goodbye.

CHAPTER 6

FAITH

Faith is to believe what you do not see; the reward of this faith is to see what you believe.

- Saint Augustine

Faith is the ultimate resource, and it can transform any experience of our lives. Faith is confidence or trust in something that is *not* based on proof.

Interestingly, we are taught conflicting precepts about faith. Life is full of these apparent contradictions. We're told "Look before you leap," and we're also told, "He who hesitates is lost." We're told "You've got to have faith," and we're also told "Trust, but verify." We're told to "Use your head," and we're also told to "Follow your heart." We're told to "Put yourself first," and we're told to "Put your family first."

We are told...	**And yet we are also told...**
Look before you leap.	He who hesitates is lost.

Have faith.	Trust, but verify.
Use your head.	Follow your heart.
Put yourself first.	Put your family first.
Put God first.	Put yourself first.
Practice makes perfect.	No one is perfect.
You're never too old to learn.	You can't teach an old dog new tricks.
It's better to be safe than sorry.	Nothing ventured, nothing gained.
Winners never quit.	Quit while you're ahead.
What will be, will be.	Life is what you make it.

I examined a host of challenges and contradictions that tested my faith and Amira's faith. We realized that things like this can happen and perhaps will happen to us in the future. Faith is not just that we get through the challenge we are facing; faith is that there's a deeper meaning in it. We have learned that it is one thing to *have* faith; it is another thing to *communicate* faith.

Faith is the opposite of fear. Anthony Robbins said, "Faith is imagination unleashed about the best possibility, and fear is imagination unleashed about the worst possibility." Can faith and fear coexist? Does living in one push the other away?

A lack of faith causes people to believe that when they feel pain, they are being punished. A lack of faith can cause people to be frozen with fear when faced with conflict. Contradictions are everywhere in our society and in our colloquialisms.

We are told...	**And yet we are also told...**
Absence makes the heart grow fonder.	Out of sight, out of mind.
The best things in life are free.	There are no free lunches.
Many hands make light work.	Don't have too many cooks in the kitchen.
Two's company, three's a crowd.	The more, the merrier.
Talk is cheap.	A word to the wise is sufficient.
Expect miracles.	Be realistic.
Fortune favors the bold.	Fools rush in.
Follow your gut.	Don't be quick to judge.
Give them an inch and they'll take a yard.	It is better to give than to receive.
Take chances.	Stay safe.

As a naval officer, I was trained to always have certainty. Naval officers always know what to do. Even when we don't know what to do – we know what to do. Naval officers never say, "I don't know what to do." We always know, especially when the path is unclear and uncharted. For us, certainty is not something that we rely upon others to give to us; certainty is something we bring with us. We walk into the room with it. If we don't know the way, we will make the way. We will find the way.

On the night of September 11th, 2001, President George W. Bush quoted Psalm 23:4 in his address to the nation: "Even though I walk through the valley of the shadow of death, I will have no fear, for you are with me." That verse guided and inspired me through the Global War on Terror and the Iraq War, and also in the birth and coming death of our son Creed.

In times of sorrow, challenge, or pain, an empowering question to ask is: "What is the deeper meaning in all of this?" It is that life is short and precious. It is that we are lucky to live in a modern nation with many freedoms, opportunities, and protections. It is that there are so many loving and caring people around us. It is that God is present. Faith is obedient action to that which God has said. We learned more about faith from our baby boy who was not even born yet. Perhaps that is Creed's legacy.

When the disciples were unable to heal a man possessed by a demon, they came to Jesus and asked, "Why could we not cast it out?" Jesus replied, "Because of your little faith. For truly, I say to you, if you have faith like a grain of mustard seed, you will say to this mountain, 'Move from here to there,' and it will move, and nothing will be impossible for you." (Matthew 17:19-20)

Faith grows in stages. Even a little faith backed by obedience will grow like a mustard seed grows into a strong tree.

We are told...	**And yet we are also told...**
Seek and ye shall find.	Curiosity killed the cat.
The higher you climb, the harder you fall.	The sky's the limit.
Slow and steady wins the race.	Time waits for no man.
The bigger, the better.	The best things come in small packages.
Nothing ventured, nothing gained.	Better safe than sorry.
Opposites attract.	Birds of a feather flock together.
Silence is golden.	The squeaky wheel gets the grease.
Actions speak louder than words.	The pen is mightier than the sword.

There are many contradictions in life, and the dichotomy we experience benefits us. F. Scott Fitzgerald, in *The Crack-Up*, wrote, "The test of a first-rate intelligence is the ability to hold two opposed ideas in the mind at the same time, and still retain the ability to function."

In *Walking with God through Pain and Suffering*, author Timothy Keller states:

> Suffering is both just and unjust. God is both a sovereign and a suffering God. These two sets of paired truths, held together without jettisoning one in favor of another, leads to a remarkably rich and many-sided understanding of the causes and forms of suffering. It also affords sufferers a great range of resources and approaches for facing it, without a one-size-fits-all prescription.[4]

The realization that suffering is just and unjust put me in a position to strengthen my faith. It allows me to have tragic joy – I am heartbroken over Creed yet can also hold in my heart and mind the joy of knowing that Creed is with Jesus.

Faith is the basis of my life, not fear. I welcome the apparent contradictions of our lives. Our faith continues to grow, and we thank Jesus and our son Creed for that.

CHAPTER 7

WORDS THAT HURT AND WORDS THAT HEAL

Then Job answered and said: "I have heard many such things; miserable comforters are you all." (Job 16:2)

Most people will not know what to say to you if you are grieving. They may avoid you. If they are with you, they may avoid the subject altogether, dancing around in conversation about nominal subjects. You may be dying inside to hear them acknowledge your situation, yet not know what to say to start the conversation that could lead to further healing.

All too often, those who summon up the courage to speak to you will say foolish or hurtful words. Most people have good intentions. Some may be trying to teach you a religious or life lesson, especially if your behavior contradicts their view on prayer or abortion.

Here are some of the inane or insensitive things that people may say to you.

"It would've been worse if your baby lived longer."

How would you know? I wish I had even a minute more with my child.

"You're lucky your baby was taken at birth."

How in the world could my baby's death be lucky?

"It's a blessing the baby died."

It's a blessing I don't slap you in the face for saying that.

"Be thankful that you know you can get pregnant."

I don't find it comforting that I know I can conceive yet end up with a dead baby.

"Be thankful for what you have."

I'd give up everything I own to have my baby be alive.

"You're young and healthy. You can always choose to have another baby."

I want *this* baby.

"Why are you so upset? It's not like you really got to know that baby."

I lost a child and you're wondering why I'm upset? I care about this baby who I got to know in my womb.

"You named your baby? Why? It was a miscarriage."

This was a life, my child, a human being. Of course I would name my child.

"God needed an angel."

I don't want an angel. God has plenty of angels. I want a baby to hold in my arms.

"I know just how you feel. When my cat died, I was upset for a whole week."

> A cat?! You belittle my grief when you compare your flea-infested feline to my baby.

"My aunt also lost a baby and she never got over it."

> You're dooming me to a lifetime of this pain? That's not what I needed to hear.

"It's a good thing your baby died at birth and not a year from now so you wouldn't be so attached."

> Attached?! My baby was attached to me through the umbilical cord. And I would give anything to have a year with my precious child.

"You should've had an abortion so you wouldn't feel so bad."

> You wanted me to kill my baby? I would regret that decision for the rest of my life.

"Shame on you for terminating your pregnancy. You made a terrible decision and will be judged by God for it."

> My baby had an impossible diagnosis, and the choice I made with my spouse is ours, not yours.

"We know all things are for the best and we just have to trust that it was God's Will."

> I want to cry out and grieve. You are telling me implicitly that if I'm not already experiencing peace over this loss, then I must be spiritually immature.

"I hope that you forget about your baby."

You want me to forget about my baby? Are you crazy? I want to appreciate and love and memorialize their wonderfully short life.

"You should try this because it helped me."

There is no one-size-fits-all way of grieving. I will grieve the way that is best for me, as I am different than you. I'm not looking for a special technique, I'm looking for compassion.

"I know some people who handled this so well, never crying or taking time off work."

Handling this well means expressing grief, not hiding or suppressing it.

"Don't fret, I knew a woman who had five miscarriages before she finally had a healthy baby."

Are you saying that I should somehow feel good that at least I'm not in her situation?!

"After a couple of months, you'll be back to normal and this will all be behind you."

I lost a baby, and you think I should be back to normal?! My life has changed, and I have changed. There's no going back to the way it was.

"You shouldn't feel sad. You should feel joyous to be alive."

Who are you to tell me how I should feel? I'd give my life so that my baby could live.

"What happened? Did you take enough pre-natal vitamins? Did you exercise too hard? What did the doctor say the cause of death was?"

Are you saying that I killed my baby? Are you trying to make me feel guilty on top of my grief?

"One of your twins survived, so you should be happy about that."

Yes, I know one of my babies survived and I'm thrilled about that. Yet I feel so horrible because their sibling died.

"So, what have you learned from all this?"

What have I learned?! What is this, a college class? My baby died.

"You know what you're doing wrong? Let me tell you."

Oh, you are telling me that how I grieve is wrong? You're trying to fix me so I can be all better?

"Just think happy thoughts."

You think happy thoughts will make me forget the loss of my baby? I feel horrible and you want me to deny my feelings?

"There, there. Don't cry. Everything's okay."

I'll cry if I want to. That's a part of healthy grieving. Don't tell me what to do, and don't tell me that things are okay when they're not.

"Just get some food in you and you'll be alright."

You think eating will make me better? I'm an adult and know when I'm hungry.

"You want to know who really has it bad? My neighbor. Their spouse died. A week later their house burned down and all their memories are gone."

Are you saying that I shouldn't feel bad because someone else has it comparatively worse? Who are you to compare my loss to someone else's loss?

"Maybe you should consider adoption so you don't have to go through this again."

Are you saying that I shouldn't pursue my dream of bearing a child because you're trying to protect me from myself? I'll make my own choices.

"It's time for you to move on."

Let me grieve in my own way instead of judging me.

"Say something instead of just sitting there quietly."

Don't tell me what to do just because you're uncomfortable with my quiet reflection.

"Well, at least you have an extra income tax credit for this year."

Do you honestly think I'll be happy getting a tax savings in exchange for a dead baby?

Here are some empowering and helpful things you can say to someone who grieves the loss of their baby.

"It's okay to have tears today." (I'll let you grieve around me in the way that you think is best.)

"You know, I don't really know what to say to you. What can I say to show you that I care?" (I'll let you tell me how I can best support you.)

"My heart aches when I see you so upset." (I care about you so much, otherwise I wouldn't feel this way.)

"I can't imagine how awful this is for you." (I know this is awful, and I won't pretend to know how you feel.)

"I want to say the perfect thing to make you feel better but I'm not sure what that can possibly be." (I want you to feel better, and I don't want to hurt you.)

"I'm so sorry your baby died." (I feel bad and won't sugarcoat things.)

"I'll stay here as long as you want me to." (I'm not going to cut out on you because I might be uncomfortable, and I'm giving you control to tell me when I should leave today.)

"I'm here to support you in whatever way you need it." (I'll be present, and you'll be in control.)

"What else do you need right now?" *Let the person answer.* "And what else?" (I'm here to help in any way, and I'll keep asking so you ultimately tell me something that would be helpful.)

"I'm going to bring some food by, and then I'm going to take care of some household chores to give you a break." (I'm not taking 'no' for an answer, and I'm going to do things to give you time to grieve.)

"I want you to know that you have been and continue to be a fantastic parent." (I'm acknowledging that your baby existed and that you are a great parent.)

"Can I pray with you right now?" (I care about you and want to help facilitate a conversation with God.)

"I'm happy to just sit here with you, even if we don't say very much." (I know that my presence will comfort you, and we don't have to force a conversation.)

"When it snows, can I shovel your sidewalk? Can I drop off chicken wings and a Caesar salad on Wednesday?" (I'm going to do specific things to ease your burden.)

Here are some things you can say to help people say the right things with you.

"I don't like to talk about myself too much, yet I really am feeling so sad about the loss of my baby. I just need to feel some love from you now. Could we talk a little about how I'm feeling?"

"I feel like everyone is tired of listening, yet I still need to talk about how I feel."

"Can I ask for your patience and support as I work my way through this?"

"I feel miserable at times, and I need to talk about my baby."

"I don't want to feel judged, yet with some people when I express my grief I feel they are judging me. I'd like to talk with you without any judgment being formed."

"Right now I need a few hours to think. Yet I do want so very much to spend quality time with you. Can we go grab a bite to eat at 6:00 p.m.? That would help me."

"Respectfully, the last thing I need right now is unsolicited advice about what to do and what to think. I'm glad you want to help. The best way to help is to respect my decisions instead of trying to influence them. Can I count on you to respect my decisions, even if you disagree with them?"

In *A Gift of Time: Continuing Your Pregnancy When Your Baby's Life is Expected to Be Brief*, authors Amy Kuebeleck and Deborah L. Davis, Ph. D. write:

> For some parents, however, advice from friends and family can feel like pressure. If their recommendations don't feel right to you, their advice only makes you feel alone. Outnumbered, you may cave to their way of thinking. Or you may decide to trust your own instincts and forge ahead anyway. Especially if you're deciding to go against strong opinions, this may further isolate you...What you may need more than anything else is someone who will listen and be a sounding board, without trying to fix or advise you. If you can find even one person, this support can be a lifeline. If can also help to remember that this is your life, your pregnancy, and your baby. It's also your decision.[5]

Realize that most people mean well. Their misguided comments may feel callous or insensitive, yet many people are not sure how to comfort someone who is grieving. They may be afraid to hurt you, so they might say nothing. Or they may recite some ill-conceived platitude that they have heard in the past. They may try to change the subject.

In *Holding on to Hope: A Pathway Through Suffering to the Heart of God*, author Nancy Guthrie describes her journey after the death of her infant daughter Hope. Guthrie writes:

> I'm not sure why, but we have this tendency to want to compare pain. This is harder than that...I think I'm figuring out that you really can't compare pain. It all just hurts.

But to tell you the truth, it hasn't been what people have said but what they *haven't* said that has been the most difficult thing to deal with.

Two weeks before Hope died, I was talking to a woman whose child had died from a heart defect at nine months of age. She told me that the hardest thing for her was when people didn't say anything after her son died. She said, "I wanted to tell them, 'How could you add to my pain by ignoring it?'"[6]

Grant well-meaning people some grace even though you may feel hurt by their comments. Be assertive and tell them how they can provide comfort or empathize with you. Tell people what you need. Don't expect someone to read your mind.

Joe Bayly, who lost three sons, wrote the following about grief in *The View from a Hearse: A Christian View of Death*:

> I was sitting, torn by grief. Someone came and talked to me of God's dealings, of why it happened, of hope beyond the grave. He talked constantly, he said things I knew were true.
>
> I was unmoved, except to wish he'd go away. He finally did.
>
> Another came and sat beside me. He didn't talk. He didn't ask leading questions. He just sat beside me for an hour or more, listened when I said something, answered briefly, prayed simply, left.
>
> I was moved. I was comforted. I hated to see him go.[7]

CHAPTER 8

ANTICIPATORY GRIEF

We must let go of the life we have planned so as to accept the one that is waiting for us.

- Joseph Campbell

Anticipatory grief is a reaction that occurs before an impending loss. Usually, the impending loss is the death of someone from an illness or birth defect. It could also affect people with non-death related losses, such as a pending divorce, a company downsizing or pending bankruptcy, a war, or a scheduled mastectomy.

A dying person can experience anticipatory grief too. Anticipatory grief can be just as intense as the grief felt after a loved one dies.

Anticipatory grief is not simply a person getting a head start on grief. Anticipatory grief can involve anxiety, guilt, helplessness, and feelings of overwhelm. A person who expects a death of a loved one may fear being alone, changing their routine, or no longer having a social life.

There are benefits too, such as spending more time together with the loved one and perhaps other loved ones. Perhaps touching and meaningful ways to say goodbye can be planned and carried out. Getting the loved one's affairs in order can bring peace to them and save time with administrative functions after their death. Perhaps handling unfinished business with the dying person could prevent regret that more could have been said, done, or resolved.

The five stages in Elizabeth Kubler-Ross's model of grief can be present in anticipatory grief. Those five stages are:

1. Denial

2. Anger

3. Bargaining

4. Depression

5. Acceptance

Not everyone will experience all five stages of grief. If they do, the stages may not be experienced in the same order.

Our journey with Creed when he was alive in Amira's womb involved a lot of anticipatory grief. When we first received his diagnosis, we were clearly in denial. Amira especially was angry with God and with the failure of modern science to create a skullcap for fetuses.

Bargaining involves trying to explain things that could have been done differently or better. It includes a thought like, "If only I had done that sooner." The bargain cannot be completed yet it helps the person feel a little more control in a helpless situation because they can identify what could have been done. My bargaining was with God. I thought, "Lord, if you grant a miracle for Creed, I will be more faithful and quit my bad habits." We were even bargaining with God to allow us to have at least a few hours with a living Creed after birth.

There were a lot of feelings of despair and helplessness. In a poorly thought-out decision only weeks before we knew Creed would die, I took Amira to a children's carnival in Philadelphia. A wave of grief overcame her while riding the carousel. As for me, I was crushed too because I felt I had failed to make her happy. Really, it was just us grieving in different ways yet grieving together.

Our acceptance stage was punctuated by our agreement that we would allow each other to grieve in our own way. We were not going to blame the other, nor were we going to try to teach the other how to grieve. We knew couples whose relationship was torn in the aftermath of a tragic loss.

We also decided to share our journey and Creed's story to hopefully inspire others. While there is such a thing as Post Traumatic Stress Disorder (PTSD), there is also the concept of Post Traumatic Growth (PTG). For our sake, and for Creed's legacy, we needed to grow.

In *A Gift of Time: Continuing Your Pregnancy When Your Baby's Life is Expected to Be Brief*, authors Amy Kuebeleck and Deborah L. Davis, Ph. D. write:

> As you turn toward the path of continuing your pregnancy, you may feel overwhelmed by emotions and the uncertainty of how this journey will unfold. On the

outside, your condition may look unchanged, but your mission has been utterly transformed.

Tentatively moving forward, you may be surprised by the power of your emotions. You may be struck by the utter contrast of what you expected – joyful preparation for new life – and where you are now: grief-stricken and bracing for death.

But continuing your pregnancy is not only a journey of grief. It is also a journey of discovery and gratitude. In fact, it is important for you to experience both the sorrow and the joy. Your grief enables you to adjust to your baby's reality, and your joy guides you forward in positive ways that will nurture your baby, your family, and yourself. Though the roller coaster of conflicting emotions can be bewildering at times, there are no 'wrong' feelings. You are entitled to experience your entire range of emotions without apology. Learning to cope with your many intense emotions is key to your adjustment.

While this may be the most heart-wrenching time you've ever experienced, you may also find that, as it unfolds, this experience can lead you through a metamorphosis. You are embarking on a profound journey that can lead you to richer ways of being and loving. You will tap into your strengths and perhaps discover some you didn't know you had. You'll grow confident that you can survive. And you will learn that what matters most is not what tragedy you face, but how you choose to respond.[8]

With anticipatory grief, your emotions may grow stronger after your baby's life has ended. The death of a baby stricken with an illness or birth defect does not bring to an end the feelings of grief. The uncertainty may be over, yet the sadness may escalate.

There are also additional losses that coincide with the death of your baby, and those include the hopes and dreams of a bright future with the child. Earlier traumas could come roaring back, enhancing the grief and despair. Yet working through perhaps unfinished mourning can help you deal with the loss of your baby. There are many ways to cope with such a loss. None will be quick or easy.

CHAPTER 9

HEALTHY AND UNHEALTHY DISTRACTIONS FROM GRIEF

We are never defeated unless we give up on God.

- Ronald Reagan

What if we managed to experience incredible Post Traumatic Growth every time we suffer? Over a lifetime, how much stronger could we be for the ones we love? How much more capacity could we have to serve God and others because of who we've become?

It's a given that everyone will deal with loss at times in their life. Everyone has their own way of coping. Some ways may be more healthy or empowering than others. Some coping mechanisms in the short term may be healthy, yet those same behaviors can be debilitating over the long run.

Suffering does not always improve your life, yet it can. Suffering can be one of the most jarring, powerful, and effective ways to usher in change to your life. Most importantly, it is in those moments of pain and despair that we can draw ourselves closer to God.

Jonathan Haidt, in *The Happiness Hypothesis: Putting Ancient Wisdom and Philosophy to the Test of Modern Science*, refers to two basic ways of coping with suffering. One is "active coping and reappraisal" and the other is "avoidance coping and denial."[9]

Active coping and reappraisal can help us think deeply about our lives and relationships. It can identify where we pursued certain priorities so much that they became idols over what really matters. It can force us to learn and grow. I know it can help us develop a deeper relationship with God.

Avoidance coping and denial involves a person blunting their emotions or operating under the illusion that the tragic event never happened. This path can include excessive drinking, illicit drugs, infidelity, gambling, violence, and other unhealthy behaviors. Even excessive focus on work or not getting out of bed most hours of the day for days at a time can be unhealthy.

Escapism in small doses can be what we need when grieving or experiencing stress. Distractions are useful sometimes. Yet destructive behavior plus a rejection of reality will leave you worse off.

With Jesus' incredible sacrifice on the cross as the supreme example for us, we can find a light in the darkness of suffering by choosing to grow and become closer to God. A tragic event can rearrange our beliefs about how much control we really have in our lives, and it can give us the reassurance to trust in God instead of trying to control everything around us.

Tim Keller, in *Walking with God through Pain and Suffering*, writes:

> Suffering removes the blinders. It does not so much make us helpless and out of control as it shows us we have *always* been vulnerable and dependent on God. Suffering merely helps us wake up to that fact and live in accordance with it.
>
> Suffering also leads us to examine ourselves and see weaknesses, because it brings out the worst in us. Our weak faith, sharp tongues, laziness, insensitivity to people, worry, bitter spirit, and other weaknesses in character will become evident to us (and others) in hard times. Some of us are too abrasive, critical, and ungenerous. Some are impulsive and impatient. Others are argumentative, stubborn, and poor listeners. Many people have a great need to control every situation. Some are simply too fragile and self-pitying when discomfited over anything. Suffering will throw these inner flaws into relief during times of stress in a way that enables us to get out of denial and to begin working on them.
>
> Second, suffering will profoundly change our relationship to the good things in our lives. We will see that some things have become too important to us. When we are devastated by a career reversal, there is real loss and grief. But we may also come to see that the magnitude of our suffering is due to the excessive

weight we put on our job status or other achievements for our own self-worth. The reversal can be a unique opportunity to invest more of our hope and meaning in God and family and others. This effectively fortifies us against being too cast down by future reversals. It also brings us new sources of joy we were not tapping before.

Third, and most of all, suffering can strengthen our relationship to God as nothing else can. C.S. Lewis's famous dictum is true, that in prosperity God whispers to us but in adversity he shouts to us. Suffering is indeed a test of our connection to God.[10]

Amira and I consciously chose to make ourselves stronger and better even in the midst of the anticipatory grief that we felt. We were blessed with enough self-awareness to recognize that we should engage in healthy behaviors. I thought, "What would Creed think of me, and us, if we allowed our relationship to deteriorate because of this? What would God think of me if I chose to become bitter and hopeless in the face of suffering?" Those thoughts pushed me in the right direction.

Our adversity made me more humble, more compassionate, and less judgmental. Creed had a piece in teaching me to be a better man.

CHAPTER 10

CREED'S PURPOSE

And we know that for those who love God all things work together for good, for those who are called according to his purpose. (Romans 8:28)

If you are in the world, then God expects you to do good things for people around you. But what does God expect of a baby who is going to die at birth? Can an unborn infant have a purpose?

When I have asked people to tell me more about their purpose in life, I have received many muddled responses that largely indicate that they are unclear about their purpose. To many, a purpose is something they make so lofty or convoluted that they cannot go to bed each night with a sense of satisfaction that they lived their purpose that day.

Amira recently said:

> Some people go through their whole lives and are searching but can never seem to find their purpose. Their life's mission is to figure it all out – to figure out their purpose. Then there are those who live their life

and look for a meaning in every experience. They look for a reason for every experience.

Then there are those who never make it outside of the womb. They have a heartbeat; a growing body; blood circulating through their veins. It's almost unimaginable that they can have purpose inside of the womb, yet they will not live on the outside. Because they are alive, we believe that they are meant for something great. Our son Creed lived his purpose and lived it well. He did not live life as we know it, but he lived purpose. This begs the question what's the definition of purpose.

Your purpose is your personal mission statement. It is your Big Why; your raison d'etre; how you intend to make your mark on the world.

There is a palpable aliveness in people who know and live their purpose every day. They are moving toward something and not simply going through the mundane motions of daily life. I believe that a purpose should be simple and something that can actually be achieved each day. Knowing your purpose produces clarity and accelerates progress toward your goals. More importantly, the knowledge and satisfaction that you live out your purpose every day is priceless.

As Christians, our purpose is in Christ alone. God wants a kingdom of God-glorifying beings. Our sole purpose of existing is to be a reflection of God's truth, goodness, and beauty. We are called to steward His kingdom. Every person is intended for the purpose of reflecting God in the world, even if this purpose is never fully realized.

Shortly after Creed's devastating diagnosis and our recognition of the reality of it, Amira and I believed that telling his story would bring others closer to Jesus.

If the first thing that Creed saw when he opened his eyes was the face of Jesus, then what more could I ask for? If a great desire, if not *the* great desire of Christian parents, is to have their children join Jesus in Heaven, then my biggest desire has been met. Sometimes it feels like winning a consolation prize, since I would give up all my money just to have a day with a healthy Creed. Yet sometimes I feel like I should be joyous without having to manufacture a false feeling of joy. The support we received from others helped give us peace.

During Creed's time in Amira's womb, we were touched by the countless comments about Creed from people we knew and from strangers. People approached us in church. We received public and private messages on social media. People sent us emails. Others mailed us books or cards. People called or connected via video. Some delivered meals. A friend helped raised funds to help support medical and burial costs. Our workplace held a dinner fundraiser. We were lifted up in so many ways. More importantly, Creed's story inspired others.

Amira recently stated:

> Creed's story changed lives. People went to their knees begging God for Creed's life. Other people came alongside us and lifted us up.
>
> Creed's purpose was to make God's name known. He didn't need to be outside of the womb to do that. His purpose was to draw others to Jesus and bring people

to their knees in prayer over him. Creed's purpose gave God an opportunity to shower His grace on us. Creed's purpose showed me the love of God like nothing ever has. It showed me that God can meet me in the worst of times. Creed's purpose showed me that I'm not forgotten; that God is still on His throne. I didn't feel it in the moment, yet I experienced that over time. You have to enter into the pain in order to really be redeemed, to experience the redemption of the pain. You can't snap your fingers and feel better. You have to get into the grief to see the glory.

In knowing that Creed had a purpose greater than himself – even if it were not in the sense that many of us know purpose to be – Amira and I discovered more meaning for our own lives.

Deborah L. Davis, Ph.D. writes in *Empty Cradle, Broken Heart*:

> Eventually, when you are ready, you may recognize something positive from the experiences surrounding your loss. Perhaps you will find you have a strengthened marriage, deepened friendships, increased personal awareness, greater confidence or better understanding of and willingness to help others who experience loss. You may even have a new baby, who might not have been conceived if the other baby had lived. These positive things do not make up for your baby's death, but you may derive some small comfort from them. Your own philosophies and outlook on life may determine whether you eventually find comfort in

recognizing anything positive from the tragedy of your baby's death.[11]

After a few years of trying to become pregnant following Creed's death, Amira gave birth to our twin girls Alexis and Ashley in March 2018. Had Creed lived, and with us being in our forties, we probably would not have had any additional children. Creed's life and death charted a course that led us to Alexis and Ashley.

I realized that in challenging times, it is not so much about pondering what to do but realizing who can I become through all of this. And then it comes down to deciding who to serve. As it says in the Book of Joshua:

> And if it is evil in your eyes to serve the Lord, choose this day whom you will serve, whether the gods your fathers served in the region beyond the River, or the gods of the Amorites in whose land you dwell. But as for me and my house, we will serve the Lord. (Joshua 24:15)

CHAPTER 11

DEATH FOLLOWED BY BIRTH

There is a unique pain that comes from preparing a place in your heart for a child that never comes.

- David Platt

It was time. Creed couldn't stay in Amira's womb indefinitely. The birth plan that we had developed with the team at the Maternal Fetal Medicine (MFM) clinic called for Amira to have her labor induced so she could ideally give birth on December 18th. Amira asked our primary MFM doctor, Joanne Quinones, to help deliver Creed.

As planned, Amira and I arrived at the hospital just before midnight on December 17th. Posted on our door at the Mother-Baby unit was a photo of a leaf floating on the water, which apparently notified staff that this pending childbirth would not be a joyous one like the other ones in the unit. Our mostly sleepless night was made as comfortable as possible by a tireless nurse named Tonya Kemp.

Throughout the day on December 18th, various medical professionals checked in on Amira and Creed. We recorded the sound of Creed's heartbeat. Amira was given medication for labor induction. The plan was to have Dr. Quinones deliver Creed late that evening.

My mother Huong and my three youngest siblings – Trung, Hong, and Thang – stopped by to visit. Amira's parents, Al and Helen Harb, arrived from Tennessee. Larry and Deb Christensen also came into town to be with us. Larry had presided over our wedding earlier that year. Amira had served in Cru in New York for years under the leadership of Larry and Deb.

A few minutes after 7:00 p.m., I called our pastor, Jack Groblewski. He was the senior pastor and a founding elder of New Covenant Christian Community Church. Pastor Jack – affectionately known by his childhood nickname Grubby by many in the church – and his wife Trish had prayed over us privately and in church services. Earlier that month, Amira told Pastor Jack that she would like him to share holy communion with us at the hospital in the hours before Creed's birth. Part of me was surprised when Pastor Jack answered my call and said he would leave his home for the hospital right away.

Pastor Jack had skipped a Christmas party just to wait for a possible call from us. It took only 20 minutes for him to arrive in our hospital room. With family and friends present, Amira and I felt reassured in that moment. Pastor Jack shared communion with Amira and me, our family members, and the medical staff who were present. A few weeks later in a sermon, Pastor Jack would smile broadly and call it "so unprofessional" that the medical professionals took communion with us.

Our visitors then headed out for the evening. As the night wore on, Amira's cervix had not dilated the necessary 10 centimeters for her to give birth. It became apparent that Creed would not be born on December 18th.

At 2:15 a.m. on December 19th, the physician anesthesiologist administered an epidural to create a band of numbness in Amira's midsection. At 2:45 a.m. Dr. Quinones checked on Amira, and we could still hear Creed's heartbeat. Amira and I anticipated that Creed would be born alive later in the day. We longed to hold him until his body completely shut down, which could be within minutes or a few hours after birth. I fell asleep on the couch next to Amira around 3:30 a.m. She dozed off around 5:00 a.m.

At 6:25 a.m. Amira and I were roused by Dr. Quinones and a nurse. The nurse moved the heartbeat detector around on Amira's abdomen, and I expected to hear the familiar boom-boom-boom of Creed's heart as it pounded away at 130 to 150 beats per minute. What I heard instead was static.

Amira raised her hands over her head. I held her hands as we imagined that perhaps Creed had simply moved around, out of range of the device. We had not anticipated that Creed could have died in her womb. Dr. Quinones said she was running out to obtain a portable ultrasound device. Moments later, she returned as the nurse gave up on trying to find a heartbeat. The portable ultrasound looked like a big, white clamshell cellphone. Dr. Quinones conducted the scan. Given the absolute silence, Amira and I sensed what was coming.

With her hands still raised over her head, Amira said, "He's dead."

Dr. Quinones replied, "I'm sorry." It was 6:35 a.m.

And we knew.

There wasn't much more to say after that. Dr. Quinones and the nurse left the room to give us space. We cried and held each other, bewildered that life on earth for Creed was over. In one sense, we shouldn't have been shocked, as we fully expected Creed to die in our arms after childbirth.

Throughout the pregnancy, I thought of how amazing it would be to hold Creed in my arms while he breathed and wiggled and perhaps gurgled. I thought of seeing Amira holding him. I envisioned my mother, Amira's parents, and some of my siblings holding him. But he was already gone. And Amira still had to go through the rigors of childbirth. What a cruel way to become a mother.

The statistics show that around 1 in about 160 babies in the U.S. are stillborn.[12] I thought of all the parents in human history who experienced the same thing that Amira and I were experiencing. What an odd fraternity of fathers I had entered.

All the urgencies of business melted away, and I didn't care if a call went unreturned or if an email were ignored.

Amira talked with her mother by phone, and I talked with mine. We broke the news that Creed had died in utero. Since we had an army of prayer warriors and dear friends anxiously awaiting word of Creed's birth, I conjured up a Facebook post to tell people in a blanket fashion that Creed had died. It read:

> Our baby boy Creed Daniel DeSa died in Amira's womb today, sometime between 2:45 a.m. and 6:30 a.m. We

had listened to Creed's heartbeat at 2:45 a.m. just before the doctors utilized a Foley balloon catheter and an epidural anesthesia in preparation for delivery. Apparently the rigors of labor were too much for Creed's fragile body. Perhaps God wanted to spare Creed the trauma of childbirth. At 6:35 a.m. the doctors could not detect a heartbeat, and an ultrasound confirmed that Creed had passed away. Please pray for Amira, as she still has to go through the pain of delivery today. We thank you for your prayers and love. Creed was the subject of so much prayer, and his short life touched many. Creed is in the arms of Jesus, and we hope to join him one day.

Our family members plus Larry and Deb arrived in the room later that morning. Everyone wanted to wait throughout the day until Amira could give birth.

At about 1:40 p.m., Amira started the final stage of labor. She was glorious as a mother, as only a mother can know. She summoned the strength and focus to give birth to a lifeless Creed. Nurse Rachel Hoffman, who we had met at a childbirth class the previous month, skillfully handled multiple tasks as the doctor carefully pulled out Creed's body. The official time of birth was 2:25 p.m. Hoffman cleaned him gently, as his skin was frayed and bruised.

Creed's body was 17 inches long and weighed 4 pounds, 3 ounces. After taking handprints and footprints, Hoffman wrapped him up and handed Creed to Amira. The organization Now I Lay Me Down to Sleep graciously sent a photographer to take remembrance photos. He entered the room at that time to handle the grim and poignant job of memorializing this moment for us.

Amira's mother and father held Creed. I called in my mother to hold him. When my mother came into the hospital room, I offered to let her hold Creed's body but she first went to Amira to hold her and cry tears with her. Amira had entered the sorority of mothers. My mother, with 11 children and also two miscarriages, was a decorated member of that sorority.

Amira and I went to sleep that night in the hospital room, and we opted to have Creed's body rest in the crib next to her. As the sun came up the next morning – a Sunday – for a split second I imagined that Creed was alive and well. I pictured a typical Sunday morning in which the three of us could wake up slowly, enjoy a big breakfast, and leisurely get dressed for church. My reverie ended there. We would have to go home this Sunday morning without a baby. That would be especially hard for Amira.

Nurse Tonya Kemp, who had cared for us the first night of the hospital stay, was back to assist us. To stretch her legs, Amira went for a walk around the Mother-Baby unit with me. When we returned to the room, Tonya was cradling Creed's body as if he were still alive. She had stayed with him the entire time we were gone.

Amira and I packed up our personal belongings. We did not want Creed's body to be left alone. A nurse escorted Creed's body to an elevator to go down to the hospital's morgue. As she was going down in the elevator to the lower level, a man entered from the ground level. He was the mortician who was volunteering his time and money to transport Creed. He asked the nurse if the body she was carrying was the DeSa baby. She said yes and asked for his credentials. Upon producing them and completing some paperwork, he was granted custody of the body. He helped transport the body to Amira's hometown of Knoxville, Tennessee for burial. Creed's body was never left alone. I found that comforting.

Amira and I drove home that Sunday. The next day we flew to Knoxville. After a short gravesite service with close family and friends on December 22nd, we buried Creed. Our unyielding belief through the fog of sadness was that Creed was welcomed into the arms of Jesus. What more can a parent wish for their child?

In the end, Death did not win. Yet it sure felt like a loss.

CHAPTER 12

DON'T WASTE THE PAIN

Out of suffering have emerged the strongest souls; the most massive characters are seared with scars.

- Khalil Gibran

For I consider that the sufferings of this present time are not worth comparing with the glory that is to be revealed to us. (Romans 8:18)

Amira and I pondered many questions throughout those months after Creed's diagnosis and death.

If we believe in a God who is all-powerful and sovereign over the world and at the same time is perfectly good and just, then how does Creed fit into that?

Did God abandon us?

Why is it that some seemingly less deserving people have healthy babies, while we were robbed of ours?

Are these bad things that are happening the result of a lack of faith or a lack of good works?

How does prayer fit into all this?

When we're in the midst of pain and uncertainty, what is the easiest, fastest way out of it?

What good can come from suffering?

Even after Creed's death, Amira harbored anger toward God. Not only was Creed gone, but Amira was upset about not becoming pregnant again. Being over 40 years old, the odds of becoming pregnant again were slim. Then, a shift happened.

It was March 2016, three months after Creed's death. Amira met for breakfast in Manhattan with her friend Dee Ann Boyd. When Amira lived in New York, she attended Trinity Baptist Church. Keith Boyd, Dee Ann's husband, was the lead pastor. Keith had conducted our premarital counseling. His teaching in those sessions plus his insightful sermons helped me deepen my relationship with the Lord.

Starting about 14 months before that breakfast conversation, Dee Ann became afflicted with continuous migraine headaches. It was not feasible to continue with her job. Keith and Dee Ann had consulted a litany of doctors and specialists. Dee Ann had endured numerous painful treatments and tried various medications with frightening side effects. Nothing was working. The only time that Dee Ann did not feel incredible pain was when she slept.

Amira described her sorrow over Creed and her anger with God. Dee Ann listened, and then she stopped Amira to tell her something brilliant. Dee Ann said, "Don't waste the pain."

That conversation led to a visit with Keith and Dee Ann at their Manhattan residence to discuss in depth the concept of not wasting the pain. Amira shared that when she had thyroid cancer in 2011, she wasted her pain on anger at God. Keith and

Dee Ann helped us realize that God does not want us to waste pain. God wants us to use it in our lives so we can grow.

A few weeks later, Amira and I joined Keith and Dee Ann at the Sunday services of Trinity Baptist Church to share before the congregation the concept of not wasting the pain.[13] At the service, Keith said, "See, that's what pain does. Pain raises questions, and none more significant than questions about God. If God is all powerful and all loving, well He could do this and He should do this, but why hasn't He done this? It raises questions about our relationship with Him. He says that He's a loving father and if I'm His child I'm secure in Him, but what does this say about my security? What does this say about His concern for me?"

What Keith said next caught my attention. He stated, "Suffering produces these heavenly groanings in us, and what it is intended to do is to wean us off of this world so that we long for the next one. Suffering is intended to get us to the place where we're not satisfied with what we have here. What we really want is our inheritance as co-heirs with Jesus. In short, suffering is intended to produce hope."

Keith shared this passage from the Book of Romans:

> Therefore, since we have been justified by faith, we have peace with God through our Lord Jesus Christ. Through him we have also obtained access by faith into this grace in which we stand, and we rejoice in hope of the glory of God. Not only that, but we rejoice in our sufferings, knowing that suffering produces endurance, and endurance produces character, and character produces hope, and hope does not put us to shame, because God's love has been poured into our hearts

through the Holy Spirit who has been given to us. (Romans 5:1-5)

At the service, I said that I learned through my experience with Creed that we need adversity, setbacks, and even trauma to reach higher levels of strength, fulfillment, and personal development. People who have endured suffering generally become more resilient. They live with less anxiety. They deepen relationships with people and with God. They change priorities.

This suffering has caused me to be less superficial and to ask the hard question, "What is the deeper meaning in all of this?" And if the ultimate purpose for a parent is to know their child is accepted into Heaven, then Creed achieved his purpose without having to toil on the earth.

We learn much more when we are in pain versus when we are celebrating successes. Suffering helps detach us temporarily from the world around us to make us long for the world to come. Many people find God through affliction and uncertainty. Suffering ultimately makes us stronger, brings us closer to God, and produces hope. God wants us to show Him who we are through the power of the Holy Spirit.

Keith said something else at the service that stuck with me. He stated, "What we need to understand is that the easy way out is never a route to freedom. The easy way out is jumping from one crucible of pain into another. God wants to grow you in perseverance and in character, and ultimately bring hope. And the way that He does that is through pain. See, God is not looking to give you a way out, He's looking to give you a way up. A way to grow in hope in Him."

God is not looking to give you a way out. He's looking to give you a way up.

If you are not in deep pain now, it will come at times in your life. People prepare for a job interview, a marathon, a wedding, or an exam. Likewise, we must prepare ourselves for tough times. If our soul is strengthened, then we will be ready to make it through hard times. People will sense our strength and look to us for certainty and meaning. Our ability to endure and grow will serve others.

God indeed has a plan for us, and our growth through suffering equips us to meet that which has been laid out for us. At the service, Dee Ann said, "My hope is far more in the Healer than it is in the healing. I know that He has a plan for me and for my life and that my life is His."

When we feel discomfort because of great uncertainty, we often seek something that gives us certainty to negate those uncomfortable feelings. Sometimes we engage in escapism. Some people may drink to excess; some may use illicit drugs; some may pursue infidelity; some may pick fights with others; some may engage in other disempowering or destructive behaviors. We all have moments of weakness in our lives. All too often in our lives, we seek the fastest exit strategy to avoid pain.

When things do not go as we had planned, we typically want answers. I believe that questions are the answer.

Amira shared her thoughts on loss:

> We are also learning that loss can give a person a more accurate understanding of their own limitations. People who have experienced loss may be more grateful for the simple things in life, whereas people who have yet to experience great loss may take many things for granted. Suffering loss profoundly changes the perspective we have on the good things in our lives.

Suffering and loss can strengthen our relationship to God in a way that nothing else can.

Suffering and pain also give us credibility. Pain and God's blessings are not mutually exclusive. God can use our strengths and skills, but it's our pain that produces depth of our faith in ourselves and others. We also have opportunities to comfort others in our pain. That's how I'm learning to not waste the pain.

In choosing not to terminate Creed despite his terminal diagnosis, Amira and I chose the harder path. And we are better for it. It drew us closer to God. It gave us tragic joy.

Given that questions can be the answer we are searching for, the two most important questions in our lives are:

1. Do I accept Jesus as my Lord and Savior?

2. Do I choose to be happy no matter what happens to me?

Yes.

And yes.

EPILOGUE

On March 28, 2018, Amira gave birth to twin girls Alexis Creed DeSa and Ashley Grace DeSa. Both girls are happy and healthy. They recognize photos of their older brother Creed and say that he is their brother.

I am so grateful that we live in the United States, where we have abundant medical resources and the ability to communicate with loved ones at the push of a button. I also think of millions of young parents in far distant regions of the world who lose their child simply because they're living in poverty.

The World Health Organization (WHO) and the United Nations International Children's Emergency Fund (UNICEF) report that about 14,000 children under the age of five die every day around the world. Most die in desolate parts of the world, far from the attention of the media. More than half of these deaths occurred in sub-Saharan Africa.[14] Most of the 5.2 million deaths annually could be prevented with low-tech, low-cost care.

The number of babies who die is staggering. On the one hand, it makes my experience seem small since there are millions of parents a year who deal with such a loss. Yet, it also empowers me to go beyond gratitude to do something for others.

What happens to about 14,000 young children a day can happen and sadly will happen in the future. We must have faith that there's a deeper meaning in all of it. Thank you for taking the time to read this. Thank you for caring.

PRAYER FROM CREED'S FUNERAL

Creed Daniel DeSa

Creed Daniel DeSa changed so many lives in his very short life. If our purpose is to make God known in our lifetime, our son did it. He has changed our lives for the better and we will always love him, remember him, and cherish him in our hearts.

May all who grieve with us feel God's comfort and presence.

May God's peace and healing cover your hearts and minds. May the God who works all things for good to those who love Him and are called according to His purposes, help you all to someday (soon) see the good that has come from all this heartache. May the peace of God which surpasses all understanding guard your hearts and minds in the knowledge and love of Christ! May this time of heartache conform you all more and more into the image of Christ.

Thank you for being with us,

Tai and Amira DeSa

RESOURCES

<u>**Books**</u>

Walking with God through Pain and Suffering, by Timothy Keller

Holding on to Hope, A Pathway Through Suffering to the Heart of God, by Nancy Guthrie

Empty Cradle, Broken Heart: Surviving the Death of Your Baby, by Deborah L. Davis, Ph. D.

A Gift of Time: Continuing Your Pregnancy When Your Baby's Life Is Expected to Be Brief, by Amy Kuebelbeck and Deborah L. Davis, Ph.D.

The View from a Hearse: A Christian View of Death, by Joe Bayly

<u>**Websites**</u>

http://carryingtoterm.org/

A comprehensive website dedicated to pregnancy continuation for prenatal diagnoses of life limiting conditions.

https://childmortality.org/

A data-filled website from the United Nations and World Health Organization for child mortality estimates.

http://trinityny.buzzsprout.com/32847/375669-all-roads-lead-to-romans-don-t-waste-the-pain?play=true

The audio recording of the Don't Waste the Pain interview.

https://www.nowilaymedowntosleep.org/

An organization that offers each family experiencing the death of a baby the healing power of remembrance.

ABOUT THE AUTHOR

Tai A. DeSa grew up in Stroudsburg, Pennsylvania, the son of Thomas and Huong DeSa. Tai is the oldest of 11 children. He was the valedictorian of the Class of 1993 at Notre Dame High School in East Stroudsburg. He then earned a Bachelor of Science in Economics degree from the Wharton School at the University of Pennsylvania in 1997.

After graduating from college, Tai joined the United States Navy. He completed Officer Candidate School and was commissioned as an officer in January 1998. He served on the aircraft carrier USS Kitty Hawk, completing multiple deployments in the Arabian Gulf and Pacific Ocean. Tai then served with the Defense Intelligence Agency Directorate of Operations, conducting various operations in Asia and Eastern Europe. He later served with the Navy's Fifth Fleet headquarters for the beginning of the Iraq War.

Tai and his wife Amira operate real estate brokerage businesses in Pennsylvania and Tennessee. They are active real estate investors in both states. Tai has authored several books on real estate. Tai and Amira enjoy raising their twin daughters Alexis and Ashley.

ACKNOWLEDGEMENTS

First and foremost, I thank my beautiful wife Amira. What a journey it has been to this point, and what a journey it will be from here. I am grateful for my twin daughters Alexis and Ashley. And of course, thank you to my parents who influenced me to be the person I am today. Thank you to my siblings: Sa, Truc, Tri, Van, Tam, Trinh, Thanh, Trung, Hong, and Thang. Thank you to Amira's parents, Al and Helen Harb, for keeping an eye on Alexis and Ashley when I needed time to work.

To my son, Creed Daniel DeSa, who is with Jesus in Heaven.

Please pray for Dee Ann Boyd to be healed. Her debilitating headaches continue. Thank you to Keith Boyd for such insightful teaching about Jesus.

Hugs and kisses to Clarence and Myra Richardson, and their son Mikey. I imagine that Creed and Faith became friends in Heaven.

Thank you to Larry and Deb Christensen for your presence, your humor, and your love.

Thank you to Jack "Grubby" Groblewski and his wife Trish for all the support, love, and teaching during that season with Creed. We are forever grateful for the attention you gave to us.

We thank Dr. Joanne Quinones and her team at Maternal Fetal Medicine for being so supportive during Amira's pregnancy with Creed.

Thank you to nurses Tonya Kemp and Rachel Hoffman, along with a number of their colleagues, who tirelessly cared for us during the hospital stay.

Thank you to Brian and Christi Fields for your friendship and your time. Thank you to Brian for ministering over Creed's funeral.

A deep gratitude for Jessica Geren and Jessica Vooz for your respective fundraising efforts to help us deal with the monetary costs.

And thank you to the innumerable family, friends, co-workers, and strangers who donated, prayed, supported, and loved all of us.

NOTES

1 Deborah L. Davis, Ph.D. 1996. *Empty Cradle, Broken Heart.* Golden, Colorado: Fulcrum Publishing, p. 66.

2 Timothy Keller. 2013. *Walking with God through Pain and Suffering.* New York, New York: Penguin Random House LLC, p. 6.

3 Amy Kuebelbeck and Deborah L. Davis, Ph.D. 2011. *A Gift of Time: Continuing Your Pregnancy When Your Baby's Life Is Expected to Be Brief.* Baltimore, Maryland: The Johns Hopkins University Press, p. 48.

4 Keller. *Walking with God through Pain and Suffering*, p. 130.

5 Kuebelbeck and Davis. *A Gift of Time*, p. 45.

6 Nancy Guthrie. 2004. *Holding on to Hope: A Pathway Through Suffering to the Heart of God.* Carol Stream, Illinois: Tyndale House Publishers, Inc.

7 Joe Bayly. 2014. *The View from a Hearse: A Christian View of Death.* (Rev. ed.) Bloomington, Indiana: Clearnote Press, p. 41.

8 Kuebelbeck and Davis. *A Gift of Time*, p. 53-54.

9 Jonathan Haidt. 2006. The Happiness Hypothesis: Putting Ancient Wisdom and Philosophy to the Test of Modern Science. New York, New York: Basic Books.

[10] Keller. *Walking with God through Pain and Suffering*, p. 130.

[11] Davis. *Empty Cradle, Broken Heart,* p. 90-91.

[12] Centers for Disease Control website on Stillbirth. https://www.cdc.gov/ncbddd/stillbirth/index.html

[13] Keith Boyd. April 24, 2016. *All Roads Lead to Romans: Don't Waste the Pain.* http://trinityny.buzzsprout.com/32847/375669-all-roads-lead-to-romans-don-t-waste-the-pain?play=true

[14] United Nations Inter-agency Group for Child Mortality Estimation (UN IGME), 'Levels & Trends in Child Mortality: Report 2020, Estimates developed by the United Nations Inter-agency Group for Child Mortality Estimation', United Nations Children's Fund, New York, 2020.

www.ingramcontent.com/pod-product-compliance
Lightning Source LLC
Chambersburg PA
CBHW061513250726
48657CB00005B/1836